God's Healing Promises

(31 days healing declarations)

God's Healing Promises

Joy Mowete

DEDICATION

I dedicate this book to our handsome son – Chizam.

Father, thank you for your power to heal and make whole is available. It's working in Chizam's life.

Chizam, keep breaking forth. Don't stop.

I can see you. You are there.

ACKNOWLEDGMENTS

My sincere appreciation goes to our gorgeous son, Fumnanya, for all the love, care, patience and support you give to your brother. We love you and are proud of you.

To all our friends and family members, thank you.

To all the teachers of the Junior Church, of The Redeem Christian Church of God (RCCG) City of David Parish, Victoria Island, Lagos. Thank you for your unending love and support to Chizam and to all our children. God bless you. We are grateful and appreciate you all.

IT IS WRITTEN

"My covenant I will not break,
Nor alter the Word that has
gone out of My lips."
Psalm 89:34

"He sent His Word and healed them,
and delivered them
from their destructions."
Psalm 107:20

God's Healing Promises

Introduction

God's Healing Promises (31 days healing declarations) is written:

- To remind you and help you understand what the Word of God says about you living life to the fullness – both spiritual & natural.
- God loves you and is interested in your well-being.
- He wants you to obey His commands.
- He wants you to depend on Him on a daily basis and invite Him into all your activities.
- He wants you to know that there is no problem in the world that He cannot solve.

I recommend you start each day by inviting the Holy Spirit to give you revelation on the Word for the day and to help you pray. My prayer is that as you read, study, meditate and pray with the Word of God, our LORD Jesus Christ will meet you as a Healer. He will touch you, you will receive your healing and He will perfect all that concerns you in Jesus name. Amen.

DAY 1

Exodus 15:26

"And said, "If you diligently heed the voice of the LORD your God and do what is right in His sight, give ear to His commandments and keep all His statutes, I will put none of the diseases on you which I have brought on the Egyptians. For I am the LORD who heals you."

I declare and decree according to the Word of God in the book of Exodus 15:26,

I heed diligently (carefully) to the voice of the LORD my God.

I do what is right in the sight of God.

I give my ear to His commandments.

I keep all His commands.

The LORD will put none of the diseases of the Egyptians on me, for the LORD is the One who heals me in Jesus name.

DAY 2

Isaiah 53:5

"But He was wounded for our transgressions. He was bruised for our iniquities, the chastisement for our peace was upon Him, and by His stripes we are healed."

I declare and decree according to the Word of God in the book of Isaiah 53:5,

My LORD Jesus Christ, you were wounded for my transgressions (sins)

You were bruise (beaten to pieces) for my iniquities.

The chastisement of my peace was upon you and by your stripes I am healed in Jesus name.

DAY 3

1 Peter 2:24-25

"Who Himself bore our sins in His own body on the tree, that we, having died to sins, might live for righteousness - by whose stripes you were healed. For you were like sheep going astray, but have now returned to the Shepherd and Overseer of your souls."

I declare and decree according to the Word of God in the book of 1 Peter 2:24-25,

Jesus Christ bore my sins in His own body on the tree. Sin has no dominion over me. I am the righteousness of God through Jesus Christ. By your stripes, LORD Jesus Christ, I am healed.

I was like a sheep going astray, but I have now returned to my LORD Jesus Christ, the Shepherd and Overseer of my soul, never to be parted from Him again in Jesus name.

DAY 4

Proverbs 4:20-22

"My son, give attention to my Words: incline your ear to my sayings. Do not let them depart from your eyes. Keep them in the midst of your heart, for they are life to those who find them and health to all their flesh."

I declare and decree according to the Word of God in the book of Proverbs 4:20-22,

I give attention to the Word of God.

I incline my ear to the sayings of God.

I do not allow the Word of God depart from my eyes.

I keep them in the midst of (within) my heart.

The Word of God is life to me and health (healing, wholesome) to my flesh in Jesus name.

DAY 5

Psalm 34:18

"The LORD is near to those who have a broken heart, and saves such as have a contrite spirit."

I declare and decree according to the Word of God in the book of Psalm 34:18,

The LORD is close to me.

He upholds me with His right hand of righteousness.

The LORD is merciful to me.

He forgives all my sins.

He is my Healer.

He is my Saviour.

My God is with me in Jesus name.

DAY 6

Acts 3:19

"Repent therefore and be converted, that your sins may be blotted out, so that times of refreshing may come from the presence of the LORD."

I declare and decree according to the Word of God in the book of Acts 3:19,

The LORD is with me.

I am sorry for all my sins.

Please forgive me.

Blood of Jesus, blot out all my sins, all my transgressions and all my iniquities.

Jesus Christ is my LORD and Saviour.

The Presence of God is with me and I am refreshed (revived) in Jesus name.

DAY 7

Psalm 107:20

"He sent His Word and healed them and delivered them from their destructions."

I declare and decree according to the Word of God in the book of Psalm 107:20,

The Word of God is life.

The Word of God holy.

He sent His Word to me and I receive it.

It healed me (cured me, made me whole) and delivered (preserved, saved, released) me from destructions in Jesus name.

DAY 8

Isaiah 58:11

"The LORD will guide you continually and satisfy your soul in drought and strengthen your bones. You shall be like a watered garden and like a spring of water whose waters do not fail."

I declare and decree according to the Word of God in the book of Isaiah 58:11,

The LORD is my guardian.

He will continually guide me.

He satisfies my soul in drought.

He strengthens my bones.

My life is like a watered garden and a spring of water whose waters do not fail in Jesus name.

DAY 9

Proverbs 17:22

"A merry heart does good, like medicine, but a broken spirit dries the bones."

I declare and decree according to the Word of God in the book of Proverbs 17:22,

I am happy and glad.

I am cheerful.

I have peace of mind.

I am full of life.

The joy of the LORD is my strength.

I have a merry (joyful, rejoicing) heart

in Jesus name.

DAY 10

2 Kings 5:14

"So he went down and dipped seven times in the Jordan, according to the saying of the man of God; and his flesh was restored like the flesh of a little child, and he was clean."

I declare and decree according to the Word of God in the book of 2 Kings 5:14,

I am obedient to the commands of God.

Father, as I read and declare your Word, I command every sickness in my body, soul and spirit to go right now in Jesus name.

I declare divine restoration and wholeness over my life and all that concerns me.

I am cleansed by the blood of Jesus Christ.

I am whole in Jesus name.

DAY 11

James 5:16

"Confess your trespasses to one another, and pray for one another, that you may be healed. The effective, fervent prayer of a righteous man avails much."

I declare and decree according to the Word of God in the book of James 5:16,

I have sinned against the LORD.

LORD I am sorry for different ways I have transgressed against you, please forgive me.

By your mercy, help me not to sin again.

By your stripes Lord Jesus Christ, I am healed.

I am effective and fervent in the place of prayer. I am the righteousness of God through Jesus Christ.

My prayer avails much in Jesus name.

DAY 12

3 John 1:2

"Beloved, I pray that you may prosper in all things and be in health, just as your soul prospers."

I declare and decree according to the Word of God in the book of 3 John 1:2,

I am the beloved of the LORD.

I prosperous in all things.

I am successful in all I do.

I am in excellent health.

My health prospers (physically) just as my soul prospers (spiritually) in Jesus name.

DAY 13

Acts 10:38

"How God anointed Jesus of Nazareth with the Holy Spirit and with power, who went about doing good and healing all who were oppressed by the devil, for God was with him."

I declare and decree according to the Word of God in the book of Acts 10:38,

I am anointed by God with the Holy Spirit and power.

I go about doing good.

I am healed of every diseases and afflictions. The Almighty God is with me.

In the name of Jesus Christ, I pray for the oppressed and they are delivered. I am a vessel unto honor in the hand of God in Jesus name.

DAY 14

Acts 3:6

***"Then Peter said, "Silver and gold I do not have, but
what I do have I give you: In the name of Jesus
Christ of Nazareth, rise up and walk."***

I declare and decree according to the Word
of God in the book of Acts 3:6,

My Lord Jesus Christ is with me.

Silver and gold I do not have, but I have the
name of my Lord Jesus Christ.

In the name of Jesus Christ of Nazareth, I
arise and walk out of every disease and
sickness. I arise and walk out of every
negative situations.

I arise and walk in the glory of the LORD in
Jesus name.

DAY 15

Malachi 4:2

"But to you who fear My name, the Sun of Righteousness shall arise with healing in His wings, and you shall go out and grow fat like stall-fed calves."

I declare and decree according to the Word of God in the book of Malachi 4:2,

I fear the LORD.

I reverence the LORD.

Jesus Christ, the Sun of Righteousness has risen with healing in His wings on my behalf.

He has healed me and made me whole.

I go out and grow fat like stall-fed calves in Jesus name.

DAY 16

Jeremiah 30:17

"For I will restore health to you and heal you of your wounds, says the LORD, because they called you an outcast saying: "This is Zion, no one seeks her."

I declare and decree according to the Word of God in the book of Jeremiah 30:17,

The LORD has restored health to me.

The LORD has healed my wounds.

The LORD has wiped out every negative mark on me.

The LORD has restored me to His Salvation.

I am whole and healthy in Jesus name.

DAY 17

Matthew 11:28

"Come to Me, all you who labour and are heavy laden, and I will give you rest."

I declare and decree according to the Word of God in the book of Matthew 11:28,

The Lord is with me. I am filled with His fullness.

My Lord Jesus Christ, I come to you.

You are my Comforter and my Strength.

I cast all my burdens upon you.

Uphold me with your right hand of righteousness.

I receive your rest.

I am refreshed.

I am calm in Jesus name.

DAY 18

Psalm 30:2

"O LORD my God, I cried out to You and You healed me."

I declare and decree according to the Word of God in the book of Psalm 30:2,

I cried out to the LORD, He heard and answered me.

In my troubles, I cried to you, LORD, you heard and healed me.

I have sound mind. I am healed. I am whole.

I am joyful. I have hope. I am full of life.

Thank you Jesus, you are my Healer in Jesus name.

DAY 19

Psalm 103:1-3

"Bless the LORD, O my soul and all that is within me bless His holy name! Bless the LORD, O my soul, and forget not all His benefits, who forgives all your iniquities, who heals all your diseases."

I declare and decree according to the Word of God in the book of Psalm 103:1-3,

Blessed be the name of the LORD.

I bless the name of the LORD, everything within me, bless His holy name.

I will not forget all His benefits.

My LORD is merciful to me.

He forgives all my iniquities.

He heals all my diseases.

He is loving and faithful to me.

The LORD is wonderful in Jesus name.

DAY 20

Psalm 147:3

"He heals the broken hearted and binds up their wounds."

I declare and decree according to the Word of God in the book of Psalm 147:3,

My LORD Jesus Christ, you are merciful and full of compassion.

I receive healing for every area of my life that is broken.

I receive help for every area that needs assistance.

Thank you for giving me a new beginning.

Thank you for sound mind. Thank you for wholeness of life. There is none like you.

You are my Healer in Jesus name.

DAY 21

Jeremiah 17:14
"Heal me, O LORD, and I shall be healed. Save me, and I shall be saved, for You are my praise."

I declare and decree according to the Word of God in the book of Jeremiah 17:14,

My LORD, you are my God.

Almighty God, you are my praise.

You have healed me. I am healed.

You have saved me. I am saved.

Lord Jesus Christ, completely, I belong to you in Jesus name.

DAY 22

Isaiah 58:8

"Then your light shall break forth like the morning. Your healing shall spring forth speedily, and your righteousness shall go before you. The glory of the LORD shall be your rear guard."

I declare and decree according to the Word of God in the book of Isaiah 58:8,

In the name of Jesus Christ, my light breaks forth like the morning.

In the name of Jesus Christ, my healing springs forth speedily.

In the name of Jesus Christ, my righteousness goes before me.

In the name of Jesus Christ, the glory of the LORD is my rear guard forever and ever in Jesus name.

Day 23

Jeremiah 33:6

"Behold, I will bring it health and healing. I will heal them and reveal to them the abundance of peace and truth."

I declare and decree according to the Word of God in the book of Jeremiah 33:6,

My Lord Jesus Christ has brought good health to me. I receive it.

My Lord Jesus Christ has brought healing to me. I receive it.

My Lord Jesus Christ has healed me and revealed His abundance of peace and truth to me.

I am blessed to be called by your name LORD.

I am blessed to be your daughter/son.

Blessed be your holy name in Jesus name.

Day 24

Matthew 8:16-17

"When evening had come, they brought to Him many who were demon-possessed. And He cast out the spirits with a word, and healed all who were sick, that it might be fulfilled which was spoken by Isaiah the prophet, saying: "He Himself took our infirmities and bore our sicknesses."

I declare and decree according to the Word of God in the book of Matthew 8:16-17,

My Lord Jesus Christ, you are my Healer.

You came to the world, took my infirmities and bore my sicknesses. By your stripes I am healed and made whole. By your precious blood, I am cleansed, I am purified, I am redeemed, I am justified and I am sanctified. Thank you Lord for the finished work of the cross. They are manifesting in my life in Jesus name.

Day 25

Deuteronomy 7:15

"And the LORD will take away from you all sickness, and will afflict you with none of the terrible diseases of Egypt which you have known, but will lay them on all those who hate you."

I declare and decree according to the Word of God in the book of Deuteronomy 7:15,

I am a child of God.

God loves me.

He has taken away sickness, diseases and infirmities from me.

He has laid them on those who hate me.

The Lord is my Healer. He is my Protector.

He watches and guides me.

No harm will come near me in Jesus name.

Day 26

Matthew 14:14

"And when Jesus went out He saw a great multitude, and He was moved with compassion for them, and healed their sick."

I declare and decree according to the Word of God in the book of Matthew 14:14,

I am not alone, the Lord is with me.

He is my Lord and Saviour.

Lord, as you had compassion on the multitude, today, remember me and have compassion on me.

I receive healing and wholeness in my body, soul and spirit.

I receive healing and wholeness in all that concerns me.

The Lord is my Healer in Jesus name.

DAY 27

Isaiah 14:3

"It shall come to pass in the day the LORD gives you rest from your sorrow, and from your fear and the hard bondage in which you were made to serve."

I declare and decree according to the Word of God in the book of Isaiah 14:3

It has come to pass; the LORD God Almighty has given me rest from all my sorrow,

The LORD has given me rest from all my fears.

The LORD has delivered me from every hard bondage I was made to serve.

I receive the rest of God in all areas of my life. I am joyful. I have confidence in the Lord. He has set me free in Jesus name.

DAY 28

Isaiah 14:25

"That I will break the Assyrian in My land, and on My mountains tread him underfoot. Then his yoke shall be removed from them and his burden removed from their shoulders."

I declare and decree according to the Word of God in the book of Isaiah 14:25,

The LORD has broken everything that represents the spirit of the Assyrian in my

life in Jesus name.

The LORD has destroyed every evil in my life in Jesus name. Every yoke is removed from me. Every burden is removed from my shoulders in Jesus name.

I am free in the name of Jesus. I am blessed and highly favored. I will fulfill all God's plans and purpose for my life in Jesus name.

DAY 29

Ezekiel 36:25

***"Then I will sprinkle clean water on you, and you
shall be clean: I will cleanse you from all your
filthiness and from all your idols."***

I declare and decree according to the Word
of God in the book of Ezekiel 36:25,

The LORD has sprinkled me with clean water
and I am clean.

He has cleansed me from all my filthiness and
from everything that represents idols in my
life and I am cleansed.

The LORD is my Creator and my Maker.

Only Him I will serve all the days of my life

in Jesus Name.

DAY 30

1 Peter 5:7

"Casting all your care upon Him, for He cares for you."

I declare and decree according to the Word of God in the book of 1 Peter 5:7,

The Lord is my Comforter.

My Father in heaven, I bless your holy name.

I come before your throne of glory and I cast all my cares upon you.

Thank you Lord, for your love for me.

Thank you for caring for me in Jesus name.

DAY 31

Psalm 30:11

"You have turned for me my mourning into dancing, you have put off my sackcloth and clothed me with gladness."

I declare and decree according to the Word of God in the book of Psalm 30:11,

The LORD is with me.

He has turned my life around.

He has turned my mourning into dancing.

My LORD has put off my sackcloth and clothed me with gladness, with mercy, with peace and with love.

The LORD has filled my life with joy and I will rejoice always in Jesus name.

Other books by the author:

I Know who I am in Christ Jesus

(Biblical Confessions for 365 Days)

Biblical Portrait of the Woman

(60 days scriptures for a Praying Woman)

God's Divine Provision

(31 Days Scriptural Declarations for Provision)

Coming soon:

Total Deliverance

(31 Days Scriptures for Total Deliverance)

Inner Peace

(90 Days Scriptural Declarations of God's covenant of peace with me)

Living Under God's Covering

(90 days biblical declarations for protection)

Exercising Divine Authority

(90 days scriptural declarations for Healing, Provision & Deliverance)

Have you been blessed with our book(s)?

Do you have any suggestion or comment?

We would love to hear from you.

Please contact us: joykent@declarehisword.com

Note

Note